12.95

Kings and Bicycles

GERARD DONOVAN

Kings and Bicycles

SALMON POETRY

Published in 1995 by
Salmon Publishing Ltd,
Upper Fairhill, Galway

The moral right of the author has been asserted.

A catalogue record for this book is available from the British Library.

ISBN 1 897648 15 4

Cover photography by Gillian Buckley
Cover design by Poolbeg Group Services Ltd
Set by Poolbeg Group Services Ltd in Goudy
Printed by Colour Books, Baldoyle Industrial Estate, Dublin 13.

SALMON PUBLISHING LIMITED

receives financial assistance from the

Arts Council/An Chomhairle Ealaíon

•

ACKNOWLEDGEMENTS

Acknowledgements are due to the editors of the following publications, in which many of these poems, some in earlier versions, originally appeared: *The Irish Times*, *London Magazine*, *Poetry Nottingham*, *Mid-American Review*, *New Statesman and Nation*, *Outposts Poetry Quarterly*, *Poetry Ireland Review*, *Seneca Review*, *Shenandoah*, *Stand*, *The Sunday Tribune*, *Sycamore Review*, *The William and Mary Review*, and *Zone 3*. Some poems appeared in different versions in *Columbus Rides Again* (1992), published by Salmon Press.

"Bog of July" won an Academy of American Poets Prize in 1993. I am grateful to the Bread Loaf Writers' Community in Vermont for their support and encouragement; for detailed and forthright criticism of early versions of these poems, I'd like to thank: Dan Giancola, Paul Mariani, Charles Martin, Heather Ross Miller, Robert Pack, Linda Pastan, and Michael Heffernan; grateful thanks also to my editor, Jessie Lendennie. This book is dedicated to Christina Nalty.

G.D.

CONTENTS

I. HOME THOUGHTS

II. LOVE SCENES

III. SUITCASE POEMS

Again, traveller, you have come a long way led by that star.
But the kingdom of the wish is at the other end of the night.

Thomas McGrath

I

HOME THOUGHTS

I knew the flowers, the stars, and the birds,
The grey and wintry skies of many glens,
And did but half remember human words,
In converse with the mountains, moors, and ferns.

– John Millington Synge

SYNGE ON ARAN

I urged him to go to the Aran Islands
and find a life that had never been expressed in literature.
— William Butler Yeats

Habitation of stone; drumbeat of limestone:
Porous broaches filled with rain.

A flint of cloud; a bicycle. Playwright
Rides above the veins of high-walled lanes,

Sails as a curragh sails on an unconstructed wave:
Creak of frame, oar-dip, drip of seaweed, hull-surge.

And always limestone. Limestone, like an intoned verse,
Rhymes down to a cliff. Yellow nests. Footfall stops.

Gulls soar in twos and threes. He kneels for the host
Of sea bird and screeching sea bird.

ON READING DARWIN IN IRELAND

Now I sit on Carraroe's coral strand, breathless after walking
   all morning,
and the hot coralbells pinch the sun in themselves;
I want to take my boots off and sleep on these dreamy skeletons
that once scuttled on the ocean bed, and I squint
until water swims across the sky and the curlew
   fades from its song;
then I am under the smooth turquoise,
watching a man lie on the coral beach,
stretching his bones on thin pink over bones;
and he slides down to me, asleep in the life of his shell.

THE CHILDREN OF LIR

This morning I've been reading *The Children of Lir*,
a story of three siblings chiselled into waif swans
and spell-blown out to dark Atlantic storms.
I learnt myths as a child in a wooden school building
with the wind in every crack. Mr. Mannion
taught us that the Fir Bolg left a coastal mist
of burning boats behind them, for those invaders
knew no going back.

And the book I read from is the same school book,
the myths arranged chronologically.
Surely those children suffered as no others,
but then all children suffer, thrust into the reflection
of their elders; they flee them with wide, white wings,
not knowing that they must come to rest on reflections
and float upon them,
their elders above and below the water.

I myself am trapped in the story, for I can't decide
if their fate was really tragic. Imagine this:
to stretch out into a gliding that fills the air
above waterfall and water lilies,
with nothing of history or memory within you,
no habit, no way of thinking;
to dream the dreams of the dead,
free from the weight of bodies that are no more
as you rise farther, and ahead

the grace of green and silver sea, plate-glass country towns,
mountains, rain and trees –
the children of Lir orphaned out of lineage,
the perfect copy that is culture.
They make no shapes in wildness, they sail alone
along craggy peaks offshore, sounding the single-string
cry of North, invading exile, renewing what is to come.

Do we feed the lost children in lakes, or watch them
at sunset by the Claddagh boats? I remember
our white-kneed wonderment at Mr. Mannion's
wolfhounds and Gaelic meter, our outrage
at three orphaned in a mute rush of wings.
I raise my hand, a man come to child,
to ask if we will recognize them
when we spiral in our own spell,
transformed without hope of redemption
to women and to men.

TWO SEASONS IN CONNEMARA

Frost stripped the hill path clean of warm entanglement
and marched its bare length along the slope
to where it met the line of sky.
Coming home again, I had no excuse
to wander from the pavement's edge;
all that was left to me was a place to go,
so I kept to the winter trail,
longing for something to get in my way
that I might break free again.

Soon, I reached the view:
in the village, a dog barked thinly,
a goose flew across the silver lake,
wings peeling the smooth surface.
Beyond, open fields and the blue horizon,
turf heaps fallen loose across the roads,
houses secured in the string of curling fence.

In summer, a narrow thread guided me through
the lean of hot seed lanterns, thorn fire, sap whip.
Still, I'd walked the path, and every step produced a cut,
and soon I traded discovery for growth:
my destination forgotten, I leaned into the mesh of air
and pitched, like water poured,
to every side but forward.

THE CROSS-MAN

I met the cross-man at his plough
working the hill field under rain clouds
that furrowed yellow through the evening.
His shirt was open to the waist
and he moved steadily, pressing earth into peeling earth
as birds wheeled black out of the turbulence
over the churned heaps of clay and stone
until their shadows dipped in blades behind him
to the single worm of soil.

He turned and asked me my sin.
I told him I could not find one
because I had no soul,
that in the valley parish below,
our acts were swallowed by the sameness of green
and the gentle forgiveness of showers.

He lay on the grass, before the steel,
and I sliced his body into thin hosts;
the wind took them over huddled stock
to tree branches and barbed wire,
holding sway in a vague dominion.

On dark Sunday mornings, remembrance gathers us
to where flowers sweeten the air
and winged song throngs the arched windows.
Pale and full of only ourselves,
we crowd the aisles with posture
to watch above the murmur of lips
the hewn tree and plaster figure;

and the old sacrifice moves across the hill
in the eternal renewal of its shadow,
and our whispers loosen to marble echo,
floating to the ear of the cold, high vaults
as spire bells fill the tilled fields.

THE SEVENTH MOVEMENT

Sundays in West Ireland
should at least be done away with
or swapped for days to live in:
no endlessness of rain on the window-pane,
no priest surviving on scant modern sin.

Even fondness cannot blur the memory:
the streets deserted, litter spiralling
in the corners of school yards, the Atlantic
whipping every blade of grass.
Even Socrates' thinking would have dropped from him
on a wet Sunday in Maam Cross.

But reveries are wasted without laughter,
and this memory has one final movement and one tune:
the neighbourhood kids,
weeping in the black fluid of boredom,
drag out a ball and kick it up the arse
of the seventh afternoon.

HARDWARE

one window admit of yellowed sign for tar soap
and hours of opening, nothing on Sunday;

one cloth bag of orange-jawed saws, mixed handle-to-steel,
tag twined through and crayon priced, one coin per instrument;

four nails, four coils of waxed rope, two pairs of rubber Dunlop boots,
a strap of belts, whalers' buckles and prongs on them to harpoon the waist
   at its true and honest dimension;

eight stacks of splinterless pine, four-by-four, and linseed oil
in rainforest green cans, coupon good for purchase to March, 1973;

five shelves of nails herded by size under hammers rotting in mid-swing,
throttled by elastic bands to the beauty boards;

one row of caulk and glue supplies, colour illustrations of use intended,
blond smile on blue kitchen background bonding a sole and heel;

three manuals for operating RCA stereophonic sound turntables,
one Brylcreemed Perry Como's jaw torn at the highest note;

one pantalooned gosoon on his toes, middle finger squeezing a penny,
head's trajectory the gobstoppers jar. *The one near the bottom, sir.*

KINGS AND BICYCLES

Growing up in Galway, I never thought about ancestry
except when gentle foreigners stuck their heads out of expensive cars,
asking directions to a town whose name they could not rescue
from the neat pages of the tourist guides;
and following my finger's gentle trace, they sailed down the boreen
into the caress of lost fields, eternally optimistic in their search
for a place just beyond pronunciation.
Once they'd found it and spent the night,
the fortress people whose ancestors would have killed them on sight
would now bring piping tea and toast and marmalade,
a gracious hostess wringing her hands, asking about their room
and if the rain *had kept them awake too long?*

Growing up in Galway, I ran from history,
ran until I'd left it far behind me:
the cobblestone paths, Saint Nicholas's church, the Spanish Arch,
husbands calling to wives lost in polyester coats;
I left all that summer touristry and walked the ocean sand at Salthill,
watching the waves build architecturally to flood my steps
    in a list of minor seas; I threw stones
    at the clouds' elastic speed;
I cleaved the water and swam and kicked till tired.

Not yet in history, Hannibal lost his way in some sorry place;
and did Paul, confused, miss the sign for Damascus?
Surely there was blood spilt somewhere in Tipperary,
a prophet killed at the well pump for his accuracy,
    burned, turned into dung and fed to pigs
    because people still wanted a little mystery?
I started thinking about the luck of conquering armies:
    soldiers, horses, pots and pans
    stumbling across town after town, exclaiming:
Oh, is this where we are?

I hoped all who came would trace their roots and be kings
and sink a pint in the pub to feel warm
and wipe the froth off their lips and even learn
Gaelic or short cuts across the words they couldn't speak.

I imagined the village crowd at the first bicycles –
circling High Nellie, High Nellie by the gate or at full speed
around every pothole and bump on the wet, brambly tracks:
lonely farmers by the hundred, all balance gone,
careering to the ground, rehearsing the voyage
to a new world of grace beyond the names they knew.
Now they could sail enthroned for miles around,
suitors of shyness and tea in every town.

Perhaps for most, love's revolution began
on a bright Saturday country morning
when the fields were ploughed, the horses fed,
the view polished, the sky straightened for visitors:
    shy bachelors in their best suits
    stuffed a trouser hem under a sock
and yellow flowers in their lapels,
then ran for speed along the lane
until they wound to distant towns
at a wobbly pace.

II

LOVE SCENES

Come with me, under my coat,
And we will drink our fill
Of the milk of the white goat,
Or wine if it be thy will.

– THE COOLIN, an old Irish lyric

FIREFLIES

Stitch of glow needles, light as thought,
weave their want in and out of the reeds
around the scent of mate; ball turret sparks,
twos and threes in the dark,
they light the world with all they know.

My boat's bright in the moon,
and you and I float in this timber pulse.
I lie on my side and trail a finger,
the water-light dies into drift,
and you lean back to where I may not follow.

Lately, you are lost in your expression,
I know only your eyes and mouth and hair.
But the fireflies have discovered our passing; they wheel
to you and me, a torch crowd of semaphore
in the dip and skid of their search
for that dark heart hidden in a single bush.

And soon they surround, and even you and I must smile
at how resolute they are;
you and I, my love, who have not learned the words
for each other's silence,
nor how to wait for it to find us.

PICKING APPLES AT WICKHAM'S FARM

The track to the trees is strewn with sweet corn sheaves;
An occasional apple bursts to its juice under wheels.
Above us, the sky, stretched to a wide blue, produces a single black cloud,
And under the red tent flapped by an ocean breeze, the aproned lady
Hands us each a paper bag and string, and we hop on Tom Wickham's
Tractor of eternal rust and trundle off to the fields.

Autumn has come low to the apple trees on Wickham's Farm;
October stirs in its shell: the ground now a crisp green, now a bruised swell.
The sky heaps in one corner wind, in another rain, and children flock
To the sunshine over the white fences, cold and hot,
Piling by the tractor on each side, accumulating into the distance
With their shrieks. We bounce to a hill
Beaded by a line of pruned apple trees,
Nothing but apple trees, in lush, tranquil arcs to the sea.

We punch out our bags and move up close;
I approach the green closet of the smallest tree,
A breeze lifts the silk of late September dust
And unbraids the leaves to crisp red patches.
Light, slanted rain flicks off my skin and spatters from the warm branches.
I reach in and grip the nearest one. It comes with a snap
And rests in my palm, and I roll it round and smell it, and put it in the bag.
I turn, but you have strayed from sight.

Somewhere, there are real words for this;
Here, in the weeks before winter, the apples are in bloom,
The evening rubs cool skin against the water, and I am busy
Plucking from the luminous canopy. That much is true.
I smell the veins, the roseate bark, the pleated
Green crank and musty shoot that drips this blotch of fruit.
Surely I could not change this moment. But already, I have begun:
The trees fall back to summer, back to spring
And I am young again, not ageing gently around the sides –
I do not feel my own steps struggle after me –
I am painless and shadowless and hang in leafy shelter –

Immersed, I look to the sound of my name.
Your smile reaches up to my arm, and slowly, firmly, draws me down.

SLEEP JEWELLERY

Outside our window, the first snow has buried the town
and paths stagger into widening drifts,
everyone skids to the amber light of home,
hissing and blowing enough to raise the dead.
The night is down and all direction's gone
and you are dozing on the couch, a raincoat on your lap,
murmuring a question to someone only you can see.

My darkness is less warm, so I go to bed with my clothes on.
The curtains are open and the moon in
and creeping dampness clouds the vision.
I sense obsidian and pyramids,
midnight funerals, bright and frozen.

Soon you lie beside me and fall asleep,
and I pray for your dreams.
My own are restless and full of lists:
I have seen the pine box,
how my insides will be out,
my dry mouth pursed,
eyes sunk into a card of skin,
hair combed from the forehead;
and my friends gone too,
all of us scattered, comfortless as a lost necklace.
Before I sleep, I wonder what it is that wakes us.

Winter mornings have a bloodless light
that fills the bedroom, but does not warm it.
For days now, a weak dawn has stained the garden with robins
and I have woken, part of human, part of frost,
breathing all the loyal jewellery of air,
waiting to feel your voice.

BOG OF JULY

Cotton wrung with wind storm, black pool and spit
And slap of peat to dry in drizzled mounds,
And noon not far off, with a cloud filling up the ditch.
Drink from the bottle of milk. We'll all be late to home,
Slathered pink, burned with sun.

We dig our way down, down to shoulder swing
To slice sod-light for November wind and rain.
Three faces bend to the shovels' stick and turn,
Three voices blend into featureless soil.

I think of the Old Irish whenever I hit deep, tangled roots –
A lake of tendrils no steel strike cuts –
Layered here, they lead me down
Past midday, to their glut, when I should be gone.

But now, summer. Dread finds no shape.
I hear you come, light-giver, in your frock,
Clutching a hand of daisies above a dance,
And I throw the shovel down and stretch my arms
Upward, towards the sun that bears your shadow.

THE SERPENT REMEMBERS

1. You Can't Touch This

Awkward, that first rental agreement.
It was time to shake hands.
No need to mention the chesty spit,
muddy fingers, the whole manufacturing bit.

Welcome to my garden. Follow me.
The tour was basic: *You can do anything here, here, and there,*
but you can't touch this.

Simplicity was the original plan,
the idea of these two wandering
among the leaves comforted Him.
But here was His one mistake:
they did not like each other.

Eve followed the pointed finger, looked at the tree,
and asked, *Why not this tree?*
If He hadn't said anything, I'd probably never have noticed it.

Adam said,
Maybe she shouldn't wear her hair so long. It hides her face.
I know she's planning to steal this apple before I do,
but I'm going to pluck it first. This is a test for guts.
After all, He brought us through all this undergrowth,
then said, *No, you can't touch this.*

The Master had created odds and ends all morning –
medicine, astronomy, a donkey –
but the two stragglers jostled for position,
each attempting to be last in line,
to trail off and then dash to the tree – a surreptitious wrench –
the triumphant dance.
Look at what I found in the bushes! Can I keep it? Can I?

2. Adam's Complaint

My friend, what have you given me?
I took the apple, the branch swung free,
the thrill is gone, and we are bored.
We have argued in the various fields –
you hit me and stalked into the grove
where lemons made yellow mist cling to the nostrils.
We swore at each other from both sides of a wide meadow,
cupping our hands to carry the barbs. Ah, property.
I have no sense for all this bounty.
And now you use it to avoid me –
you dive into the pond and surface in the deep part,
knowing that I can't swim. I wade to my knees and ask for love,
you shake your head and wave a finger.
I tried a clumsy ambush
but you got the better of that.
Now you show up with an apple.
Is there no end to the evenings that come and go,
the nights that rain pleasantly?

Lately, I have taken up a hobby:
I chisel animals into the face of a distant cave.
You follow me there and sing your songs. I roar from the ledge,
Hey, I'd like some quiet here! My complaints echo down the cliff
and smother in the daisies you link with patient refinery.

Now this apple. Clouds fill the blue and press at the sun.
My mouth closes on the cold fruit
but something warm squirms under my tongue.
I spit out a shout and reach for you,
but you are already tumbling through the flowers a field away,
calling my name, daring me to dress you.

3. Song of Eve

When he made us, the world was only promise.
When he abandoned us, there was work to be done.
Adam built the walls that were commanded built –
a simple man, he did not understand
the turn of wrath against us.
He worked until his body protruded pain
and then he died, full of unknowing.
I found him in the bushes, near the tree,
his face arched in the shrubbery, arms locked behind his back.
I stroked his hair all that morning, knew the pressure
of my own company. I felt eyes watch me,
but composed no expression. I was woman.

The Master's plan for me was subtler. I would produce,
then I would wrinkle and burn with passing years,
my body's fruit bruising me. I wandered along the walls,
the one garden many now. My belly had stretched the skin;
I thought it would burst: a tumour seed exploding into the air
and into every garden, everywhere.
I gave birth instead. One body slid down my thighs,
my screams in its ears. I washed it clean with grass;
the other followed soon after, shivering with clenched fists.
He took them both out to far fields, to where the moonlight
froze black dirt and the sky had no stars.
He would not let me near them. He was man.

4. Companionship

What did they expect?
Apples don't grow on trees.
Anyway, someone switched the lights off
and I was left in a cold garden without running water
and nothing to eat. I slept out of hunger
and fell off my branch,
spreadeagled and fandangled and breathless
and that old tongue tickling the air.

If I could, I'd laugh. I'd ask,
*Please, let me pick just one forbidden thing,
it doesn't matter what I do.*
Next, new people, I suppose.
I should call after the departing light
and suggest that I might stay;
after all, this world's my home.
Every time I ask, I hear a sigh fill up the place
and blow all the manicured shrubbery to hell;
but, with the indomitable care that made me,
a tree remains – and a warm branch and a bud,
so I slide along the wood and watch all winter long
as it ripens into *Yes*.

HAVING FORGOTTEN TO WATER
THE ANNIVERSARY ROSES

No use placing them in the window light
Or moistening the clay,
Their collapse wove a pale procession
While the King and the Queen were away.

Petals shrunk in pink mail
Kept jousting with ribbon and lance
As they fell one by one from their horses
In a splendidly random array.

And that's what you find upon your return.
The merry tournament's decayed; every pennant droops
From an accusatory corpse of thorn.
The weapons still glint, but the crowd is gone.

IN THE HOME NEAR ST. STEPHEN'S GREEN

Cut grass curves away in the window
to a late Friday lingering under sunlight.

You've been gone an hour to feed the ducks,
and I look through the railings for your hat

to bend to the beaks that strain to your touch.
You tell me they flip and show you their legs,

but it's you reliving those halycon dates
when you cycled in the grass and I ran in my suit,

never reaching the grip of your hands and press of your feet,
and your laughter under summer's leaves, drinking tea from a flask

on Grafton Street. You say the evenings were longer then,
but that's just you being generous with the past.

I can't see much now. The breeze from the sea is gold and smooth,
tinting the park with ambrosia fog,

and swallows curl to the pond glare,
gathering in an accordion upward

over sleepers drooped on benches,
dreaming of Italian lovers.

No one tells a generation it will grow old.
One wakes, and is eighty,
and the air is too cold,

and you are at the door again.
Look – you've brought Stephen's Green into our house!
The picture is here: the plant is in the corner:
the vase holds an inch of water: the mirror an inch of reflection:
the tile is yellow: the canary sings and does not know.

Tomorrow, you've promised me a smile.
Now give me that flower. We'll have to put it back.

BLACK WIDOW

Spool out the spit and sail on it,
your legs all repair at the edge of the universe.

Silk-propelled, you thresh the drum snowflake tight,
master killer, black-flag pirate, cove bound

until a shape looms and you poise at ship's side
with rope and grapple, one lip puckered under a sailor's eye.

Come, Concubine. Patter your schooner on the silver line,
pausing at every shiver to raise your hook.

Now, heave to and splash – throw the loop, tug,
timbers flexed in the struggle. Hole and sink mate

down to his brittle skin; drop anchor from weighted calm
on turbulent, bejewelled ocean,

your hull resonating in the wet applause of leaves.
Ah, your vessel's bright with dangling tackle

but I lose your shape in the wild greens
as trapped rain shreds the garden.

TWO MOTHERS

You came limping from a hole in the fence,
circled my house, one eye on mine, one on the dish
I'd filled each morning of a hot week;
you swayed, pendulous, with all cannon out and a full belly crew,
tail billowing in the wind

and lapped at your reflection,
for no Narcissus survives
that thirst.

We each kept our distance. I did not care that much for dogs,
and you had not come for company.
But today, when you did not come, I went into the tall weeds
that seethed with late spring
and found four pups cupped in the stalks of sweet seed grass,
fat and wet and dreaming milk inside them,

miles from town, and Mother gone; even flies
seemed to threaten that paste
of spiny hulls.

I trudged back to the house, thinking
to put straw in a box and place them
beneath the teat of barn's skylight.
But I found you at my doorstep, drinking water from the dish.

We must have passed each other in the long, sweltering grass:
I to the litter, you to sustenance;
one taking in, the other empty now.

THE FRENCH DAUGHTER

A slip of feet,
a dance dressed up,
and the gate swings wide to morning
and a bow-tied field.

She runs, minding perfume and a little grace,
towards the fence that has thinned
to a thread across the slope. Her body
is opening up. The Alps crowd down.

That swell to the next town suggests,
but no hurry now. There are trinkets
in every crack. The world is loose and showing
into her first full summer.

THE LIGHTHOUSE

And now, by this painter's rock, the tide is awash with seaweed,
and near the island, a few gulls tip on the wind over shallow water.
I linger by the causeway that whispers, *Don't cross*,
and stretch out instead on the sedge grass,
face to the unscrolled stars
where ancients placed their departed friends.
We talked in your flower garden a week ago,
now your voice is wind on a sightless plain
where no friends will find you.

The hills bend to stars above your easel's haunt
and the sea's rumble booms into deep midnight,
and the sand, first wave-blackened, now swirls brightly back;
but I lose everything in the beacon's pass.
You painted this scene often into the evening,
a stick figure in shadow summoning round and generous colour
to wrap Atlantic cloud, or dabbing the brush across Spring afternoons,
coaxing hues from young flowers and trickling rain-streams.

See, my friend, the earth turns without you:
small birds drench the moon and the cloud
and fasten to the night beach, feeding;
the worm curl of wash rolls them back
as the turning lamp glows strong;
it's fine to feel this loss flash
and know a fuller light is sweeping across continents
to the crack of East behind those hills.

And how the lighthouse keeper must feel time this night
with only a chair and book to give him sight;
how long the stairs to the top must wind above his tired step,
the glow hot on his face. And how fast his children grow
these stormy nights, when he shines the magnificent lamp
and they lie in bed and dream of men
who shed strong light, and warm and endless light.

III

SUITCASE POEMS

ON THE WAY TO SOUTHAMPTON TOWN

On Monday morning, driving to work, I saw from the corner of my eye
a shadow just off a curve in the road, near the pine trees.

The next day I remembered and slowed at the bend.
It was a badger, tucked into itself, some blood at the paws

and I heard the mental replay, the thump and the skid of the body
all the way to the teeth and gelatinous head, folded and prone.

On Wednesday, the wind tugged at the fur wet from a night's rain
as two crows waited on a thin branch. I blew the horn. They wafted down.

I thought about choice on Thursday, about how I might not want to see
what was becoming of the badger; how I might stare ahead, or fumble

with something at the appropriate moment, and so miss it altogether,
but the body was ripped on one side, tweaked at by a careful fist of birds

and I swerved to hit them all, every one, but thought about the mess
and saw, at the last moment, the coarse white bristles of its stripe.

On Friday, a red scrape marked the shovelled resurrection,
no more of the badger, no countdown to the skeletal proof.

That evening, I sought a myth to sanitize it all, an allegory to clear the air
and let me forget the creature who must have had somewhere to go,

and I found on a postcard the story of the saint who loved apples,
who, fearing the desire would hold him fast to this life,

set one down in front of him until it punctured with rot,
caved into worms, and he was cured.

But that roadside shade is still bearing down.
It is Saturday afternoon; I pass the mirror in my hallway

and glimpse the glassy crawl of evidence, a man with receding hair,
and quicken by, for I could not stand to watch him suffer.

AN ABORIGINE ON DOVER

An Aborigine landed on Dover Beach last winter
and claimed England for the Aborigine nation.
He parked his canoe and stomped up the cliffs to the view.
He had the desert in his eyes, stuck a flag in the ground and said,
This is ours, mate. Tapped foot, said, *Imagine a drumbeat;
we'll be along soon to divvy up the place and then you can all leave*.

Storekeeper phoned police about naked man near the beach.
Constables brought man to the cells. Attempted Invasion,
shouts the headlines. *Well*, says the Prime Minister,
we'll just have to surrender.

Terms arranged with Aborigine colonial troopers
from Ayer's place. Translator agreed terms,
Royal Family got one week to find a flat.
Queen got her own bed in Notting Hill.

The canoe Aborigine called his family from pay phone
and promised them Somerset, Northumberland, and London.
A thousand canoes rounded Gibraltar and clogged Thames.
English swam north to the Shetlands.

CHILD OF AN OLD VICTORY

First light. Scrape of *rasquado* on a Granada hill;
cracked phlegm laugh, yell coil
gather an image under the cold moon:
a gypsy grabs her hem and thrusts a knee
as the strum of dress twists in the skyline caves
where wine is perched in wicker and candles burn
in the bash and stamp of dance on damp stone.

The slender boys throw off their dirty vests and dance,
and the unshaven men who crowd the cave
crouch over guitars and pound rhythms from gut strings;
tied to her death as she disappears and all stills,
tied to her miraculous swing into the warm gleam,
notes flurry to follow her in and out of shadows.

Down the hill, I am awake, and listen, reminded
that my past is desert and Moor.
The lady rides along the sweep of morning sunflowers,
swinging her sabre above swirling silk,
taunting white stone with muscle;
she performs for crusaders in their mausoleums,
for authenticated faith stored in the back rooms of libraries;
she claps for all that the West accumulates and cannot use.
The residue inside me stirs faint visions in the blood.

By noon the sun has tightened in the sky
and the horizon creaks under a boat's flapping sail;
a long, Dorian scale climbs the stepped alleys
and winds to silence in the orange groves.
I watch women lean from balconies, calling the children
whose names drift half a street, never reaching them,

and in my rented room, by the whitewashed window sill,
I wait for rescue, child of an old victory;
but what comes is that breeze from a bright chalice sea –
the cedar branch tremors from a flown song –
the crescent-winged bird is above me,
unwrapping its flight in resumptive darts
until I have no window left, and all is empty sky.

VISITATION

I had always seen Gabriel as muscle-bound
when he balanced on the Virgin's window-sill,
his hairy legs descending to sandals,
a gym-built cherub
making space for a Divine surprise,
one muscular finger raised against dissent
—and that havoc with the furniture when he took off –
those wings skinning her straw mats from the floor,
plastering everything with wind
as they flapped him from the window
and back to heaven, his frock riding high.
Did she look? Did she shout after him,
And what if I don't?

THE LIGHT GOES ON

At 3 a.m., when the streets are silent,
when the radio has dimmed to a whisper and crackle,
I feel light brighten the cities inside me
as the silver lines of crooked roofs unfrost
and fluorescence widens the cobblestone.

The coat under the bridge slips out a finger
and draws the cardboard down,
the bent woman in pyjamas shuffles to the doorstep
and grabs the milk bottle, as though it were a lost femur
from a posture she'd once known.
Birds in the park trees burst
into broken reflexes of song.

The leaves blow across the yards, and everyone in those cities
must be surprised at how quickly the day has come,
for even in paradise, the light is off when the door's shut,
and were they not just now dreaming
of their sons in boats on diamond lakes,
of singing after six beers,
of crystal, open-mouthed sleep in deck chairs?
I know my cities, compressed in so many layers,
gold and glittering in the dark,
each wrapped and dated as I left them
at fifteen and twenty and twenty-five
as I fed and fed and fed.

Ah, each beautiful town, preserved in the lean of twilight –
the off-white spire, black bell, the vista of sea,
the market-place stuffed with lettuce and beans and onions,
the etched pottery, the grain, the muscled goats limp on a rope,
their muddy hooves drumming impatience.

Now the sleepers wake to an edge of light on the skyline
and emerge sightless in breathless rumour,
looking for the flames that hauled them from their beds;

the righteous set up shop on box tops, declaiming from open books;
the starved ones totter from the desert in loin cloths,
saying, *I told you so; now you'll be sorry; do you have any food?*
The police cordon off the spire from whence the light issues,
but no one's really sure in all that tissue.

I feel as one who had dug for years in the same place –
and now, with bare hands, sweeps away the clay
to a cross blazing in all that sunlight.
Balancing on it, I hack all around
until the earth drops away and the vista funnels to
townspeople milling in the streets below,
hands on mouths, screaming and genuflecting in waves.
I stand in slippers, in a circle of fire, on a city's highest spire,
a god come to inquire, stranded in his second coming;
and the bravest of them climb all the way up,
a starved string of heroes, calling in tiny voices for me
to grab the line and be saved.

At 3 a.m., when every city in me is a riot and raucous,
I prove that the light is out in paradise when the door's shut,
for I swing it open, and the bulb bathes my kingdoms in a rich yellow gleam.
I see no conflagration in the food,
no protest surging from crowded tenements
of coffee and ice cream.
I bless myself and reach within.

BALLAD OF THE BRIDGE TROLL

All he wanted was a coin
Pressed into his broken palm
By smiling passengers in the rain
Who came to cross the battered span.

They refused, being human kind,
And brought confusion to his mind;
They whipped their horses into haste
As their carriage trundled past.

He wiped his brow and let them go,
The two red boys in silver draped
With crescent moon and golden scarves.
They climbed the hill, and were no more.

He thought himself a coward then.
He had not chased the couple down
And beat their lily skin and slender hands
Until they paid their debt to him.

The paper horses drew the coach
Along blue mountain crevices;
The wheels folded, the boys fell out,
Their cries like popping seeds.

In storm and rain, the Troll sees lights
Douse his bridge on velvet nights
And hears sweet voices cross, unfurled,
To lure him to the spirit world.

VINCENT'S NEW IRISES

Below, they are legion: wet, black roots,
Slick tubes of attention, slanted and packed,
Fleshy wires beneath undulating fields
That spray out the surprise of small irises.
He follows his brush into the clear, rippling pasture,
Disturbs the buried reflection of pink
That holds his face. He feels under earth
For the breath that hardens into flowers,
For the chromatic sense that shapes them.
He strips the fields past clay to find
A pulse for the shivering perfume.
The wind makes stems boil in a rainbow froth;
Irises stain the whites of his eyes.
The evening sharpens into stars.

DISCOVERY OF GRASSES

From among the trees,
knees locked to a stop,

the deer watches fresh grasses
in the clearing, after dawn.

Webs draped on blades drench the eye,
dew steams from deep green

and desire circles through fear,
pressing its own fence,

wet nose in the air for all invisibles.
A breeze shifts the forest brush,

the sun climbs an hour,
a bird sings for miles.

THE LOST BELIEVERS

In my dream, I saw their steps strewn far behind them in the sand
As though unspooled from some distant order, nearer and nearer
To the rasp of their breath, and their eyes at our door, meek for water.

In my dream, their care had made them wander
Too far from the sign, and they found me instead,
And my mother washing me down with poultices,

For I had grown as thin as my suffering;
I had lain down and held hands with my guardian pain
And fallen under it, through my outline –

They stood by my bed, unfirm as the candlelight,
Drawn faces swirling in the flame,
But they slipped away without even asking my name.

I see the Magi now, figures swept along in their search,
Affixing to each alteration in the sky a rigid finger –
That star may be scabrous, or it may be Bethlehem.

COLUMBUS RIDES AGAIN

1. Red

After many years of ruminating
we've sent Columbus back
because he keeps hanging around
the basketball courts, drinking whiskey
and dreaming of buffalo.
At night we throw him blankets
but he's always gone by morning
when the sun plucks out the huge, shaggy stars
from a sky he calls the black pasture.
Later in the day, he's usually seen on Fifth Avenue
talking to himself, making stop-and-start runs
and screaming south at the mountains.
Passers-by have complained
that he keeps maintaining he was here first
and has rights (which we've explained to him).
We had one report that he accosted an elderly gentleman,
held up a necklace, and demanded Manhattan back.
We showed him how to use a vacuum, but he hated confined spaces
and took to selling jewellery at the corporate entrance
and was arrested and put in jail, where he
banged on the bars and walked himself
into a tight circle of talk.

2. Black

Columbus has not been able to accept
the concept of ownership. He asks where the others are,
the ones who cried all night in their chains,
the dark men who cut cane in Santa Domingo under the warm blue
sea breezes that dried their sweat. The castles of the morning
were made of chants they sang to get their families back.
He wants to know why we learned this skill from him and took
it up past the unforgiving Delta
and put the sails with cut holes over our bodies
and stood in moonlit fields in Southern Missouri,
ejaculating white against the sheets that caressed
the skin in the warm blaze of the cross. He says he never meant
to keep them slaves forever, because even Spaniards remembered
the power of the colour that absorbs.
Columbus says he remembers the Moor
who lived under the castle walls in Naples. He heard
the birds each morning in 1484 and woke to her body
gathering sea shells. He fingered the cold wood
of his lute and watched the gulls circle
and knew he could not trap her, and his eye strayed
to the blue line of the bay.

3. White

Columbus refuses to act white.
He hangs around the alleys and smokes. The Italian
smokes. He likes to wear suspenders and play blues guitar
and push cues in the blue halls. That is not why
Columbus is now at the docks boarding this ship.
He is being sent back
because he has not kept his promise
to stay away from the harbour and the sailing ships.
He was caught making drawings and selling them.
He denies that he drew inferences
or intended ingratitude. The canvas showed white sky,
rolling blue underneath, and a stick floating.
We roast primitive myth from the earth,
we thank God for our confinement in the States of Eden,
and this man keeps insisting that there is no edge out there,
that we can travel in a straight line
and return without turning back. We found him
breathless behind a trash can holding a torn idea.

Columbus is nearing the horizon
because we have enough mythology now.
Let him disappear in the pinprick of a sail
and contend to others that he saw another land
where there were riches and high buildings.
But Columbus doesn't know the name of race: how it navigates
through his veins – how it will
read the maps to every part of him,
then set up a frontier camp in his heart.
They will sit in their poverty and hear the shouts of a man
gesticulating by a campfire, his words
as meaningless as the shadows. When the natives
turn away from his words,
he will slaughter them.

54

ZEN MASTERS IN THE SUPERMARKET

To sit there smug, to imperceptibly smile
In bronze contentment: six fat figurines
Whose carved protrusions present a line
Of bellies ripening to a mollusc sheen
In a grove of tinted glass. Should I purchase
The gathered silk, tight between the cheeks –
Those minute curves to privacy–of the lotus
Buddhas, six grapes on cold marble, who contemplate?

I know chaos; I know dread. To be glib with fate
Is the gift of snails on a road. They charge as tinkling bells
To a crystalline enlightenment, that flux of an instant
When spirit oscillates in confusion, the burst of shell.
Strive on, buddies. No one will miss your struggle.
Practice at becoming all you want.

IN THE PLACE OF WORDS

Framed in the window, the metric of blue
presses morning's room with promise.
Along the wall, the pipe organ of books and shelves
measures a terraced, frugal time.
Across the floor, his child
fades through sunlight's glass divide.
On his desk, the faces he would recognize;

and under his gaze, those lines
curled on the page's amulet breadth
lure an image that will not come
as spell or talisman.
The making hour is done.

Before him, in the place of words,
that whisper of demons rides from mind's rafters,
lovely, nameless, circling down.

SEVEN DAYS OF DELIRIUM AND SHELLS

On the morning of the last day, we walked the strand's yellow
between green sea and green jungle; as all week, you hung
from your fingertips and left your eyes wander at your feet
until you bent to the wash and scooped a palm of foam;
it melted to a shell, empty as a jewel
except for that labyrinth of brittle sound you held to your ear,
but you laid it down to the band of other shells,
the spirals and the noon seaweed wet with sun,
and crossed the strewn nebulae, your weight a toe on every perch
you picked from the expanse of shore.

As all week, we tired quickly; then back to the hut
and the green shade and the wicker chairs; a drink,
a few pleasant words until you slept; then I read,
stranded in the furniture as the clouds moved in
and rain clapped on the roof and danced in my ears.
The island had too many stones
for bare feet, too much wind suffocating
in orange palm, our hammocks like larvae on strings
germinating dreams through the afternoon
that swelled, broke their shells, and woke us.

Light spilled away to a single moon hardened in night flesh;
my mind cleared to the silences:
the spider swoon on a fragrant branch,
the swim to the light at the edge
of the young in the grip of the sedge,
the twilight wipe of red,
the shapes strung out ahead:
birth-mausoleums, pricked with wriggling light,
the dark luminous with night.

When you woke, I made you tea in the china cup
that would travel back with us and be sipped from again
in front of the morning television or a Sinatra tune –
Oh that promise of something new! But we had found
nothing new – Oh that promise of what will remain the same!
And a hundred yards away, a million shells, crackling, sliding –
cantankerous loose flakes evangelized with sway,
the baptism's cupped flow glorious, warm, wet, glistening;
breezily naming and renaming
the rise and spill of broken crabs
as though they first rode victorious on the tide.

And the stars found our town
in its woven basket of streets, soft to the prod of our steps,
the south wind ripening fruit
around the hidden harbour,
the boats soon to click their sails in the dawn air
out to the hardened salt, peppered with swell,
the nets thrown, decked fish in labour.

We moved into the tall grasses,
separate, fragile.
The tentacles of lighthouse lost us.
But our voices survived.

LAST FARMERS' MARKET BEFORE SPRING

This is the time of the hard sell:
They cannot drive a full truck home.
They arrange their children
around the rolling red and green apples
and I almost get by.

He gives me the bundle
and picks a leaf from my hair.
The first rain in four weeks
relieves the screech of leaves on bone ground;
the glass tinkling breeze
throws fall into the late morning.
I did not know there was a sky!

By noon, the crowd loosens
to the waiting bicycles, to the line of vans.
Children press their smiles to the rear windows –
everything is sold!
All manoeuvre home as light as geese,
turning with one wrist.

ON HIS PORCH, A FARMER
EXTINGUISHES HISTORY

They're all out tonight, though I can't read them,
blooming clear and cold from the corner of the sky
where the night is thick, black and unstirred,
cast in flat glimmering stories I've never learned
   glowing steadily on my acres.
     But I do know the tales of where I live:
my tractor's a ghost in the potato field,
and by evening, low owls swoop under yawns of barn timber
and sometimes light fog rolls on a birch tree and drapes from it;
   I keep waiting on this porch for the natural world
     to shape its accidents of beauty.

I'd rather have an empty sky than old enmity.
Every clear night they trot out in turn on the dimly-lit boards:
spell-makers, bulls, Zodiac sisters,
men killed over a foot of land or banished for a loose comment,
traced for posterity, and now we're stuck with it.
   I'd bring those myth-boys down and give them work!
   Gemini on weed control, Taurus turning sod all day.

But tonight, I have rest, these beers, the sink
of froth and dreams and happiness, for my work's done and in the past.
   I lean back and skip lifetimes across the stars
     that deepen the night across my yellow crops.
My cat slaunches up to me and jumps–she's a lazy shape on my lap,
good for nothing except the moment,
each claw a point in pleasure's wax and wane.
   I stretch up to switch the porch light on –
     look, you curled dream, look up: they're gone.

INSTRUCTIONS FOR LEAVING

Wash thin stairs with water and with wine,
move to remove with your bucket and your brow

fingertips from brass and the mind,
lift sinewed curtains from the window's light-spine

and walk fearless, for all the rooms are empty
to echo till human again. The angry steps are gone,

all shouting's cleared, the silence stretches skin-calm
on so much floor and so much wall;

polish the sun into that firmament
where lives strip down to nothing at all.

Outside, the porch sings with flies in the long afternoon
crowding to a glass idea that will kill them soon.

Perhaps in this darkest hour that voice may come,
but now you languish in one corner of what you know,

for each and every room is empty,
and there is nowhere left to go.